DISAPPOINTED

by Meg Gaertner

The Child's World®
childsworld.com

Published by The Child's World®
1980 Lookout Drive • Mankato, MN 56003-1705
800-599-READ • www.childsworld.com

Photographs ©: Shutterstock Images, cover, 1, 4, 8, 10, 17, 18; LightField Studios/Shutterstock Images, 5, 6; iStockphoto, 9, 13, 14, 19, 20, 22 (bottom right); Light Field Studios/iStockphoto, 22 (top left); Wave Break Media/Shutterstock Images, 22 (top right); Michelle D. Milliman/Shutterstock Images, 22 (bottom left)

ISBN Hardcover: 9781503828063
ISBN Paperback: 9781622434664
LCCN: 2018944228

Printed in the United States of America
PAO2395

ABOUT THE AUTHOR

Meg Gaertner is a children's book author and editor who lives in Minnesota. When not writing, she enjoys dancing and spending time outdoors.

CONTENTS

RITA'S PARTY

Rita's birthday party is on Friday. She cannot wait. Her best friend Lucy is coming! They will have a great time.

5

Lucy gets a cold the day before the party.

Now Lucy cannot come. Rita feels disappointed.

She thinks her party will not be as fun.

BEING DISAPPOINTED

People want a lot of things. But they do not always get what they want. Everyone feels disappointed sometimes.

Some people **pout** when they are disappointed. They think about what they did not get. They might **blame** others.

When you are disappointed, it helps to **focus** on good things. Watch a fun movie. Spend time with friends.

It can also help to tell people how you feel. They will understand. They have probably felt the same way.

It is okay to be disappointed. You will not feel disappointed forever. You will find something else you want or look forward to.

THINK ABOUT IT

Can you think of a time when you were disappointed?

Chapter Three

HELPING OTHERS

Sometimes others are disappointed.
You can help them. You can listen to them
talk about their feelings. If they want to be
alone, you can give them space.

They might not feel better
right away. That is okay. You can
still be a friend to them.

WHO IS DISAPPOINTED?

Can you tell who is disappointed? Turn to page 24 for the answer.

A

B

C

D

GLOSSARY

blame (BLAYM) To blame someone is to say it is his or her fault. People might blame others when they do not get what they want.

focus (FOH-kuhss) To focus is to think about something or someone. When you focus on the good things, you take your mind off the bad things.

pout (POWT) To pout is to push your lips out. People might pout when they are disappointed.

TO LEARN MORE

Books

Dinmont, Kerry. *Jealous*. Mankato, MN: The Child's World, 2019.

Kreul, Holde. *My Feelings and Me*. New York, NY: Skyhorse Publishing, 2018.

Moore-Mallinos, Jennifer. *A Whole Bunch of Feelings*. Hauppauge, NY: Barrons Educational Series, 2018.

Web Sites

Visit our Web site for links about being disappointed:
childsworld.com/links

Note to Parents, Teachers, and Librarians: We routinely verify our Web links to make sure they are safe and active sites. So encourage your readers to check them out!

INDEX